RUNAWAY WORDS

Written by
Patricia Taylor

Illustrated by Wendy Leach

Hi! I'm Addi. I'm 6-years-old. I have a younger brother and an older brother.

Being a sister is a really important job. Plus, I am a younger sister AND an older sister, which makes me double important.

I love horses

and mermaids

and strawberries.

I also really love playing with my brothers
and helping to take care of them.

But I'm a little sad about one thing.
My older brother Charlie can't talk.

And I really reeeaaallllyyyy want him to talk
to me.

I asked my mommy about it one day.
She told me that he used to talk, but a few
years ago he lost his words.

I've lost a lot of things.

In fact, I'm pretty good at losing things.

But I don't understand how Charlie could have lost his words??

I'm not so sure my mommy is right about this. Where did his words go?

. . . Oh no, maybe they ran away and can't find their way back!

Well, I'm his sister. . . I'm going to help him find them!

Hmmmm. . . where to look?
I've never searched for words before.
Where do words like to hide?

Where would I go if I were words?
Somewhere dark and hard to see maybe. . .

Oh, I know! I'll look down Charlie's throat
with my handy dandy doctor's kit light.
Maybe the words are just stuck down there.

"Charlie. . .just. . . .open. . . open. . . hold still. . . .
just open . . . a little. . .just a quick peek?"

Ok. I couldn't really get a good look, but I couldn't make out any words stuck in there.

Oh! I got it!
Maybe he left his words
in his books!
He loves his books!
I'll go grab some.

"Charlie, look!
See, here are your words!
Remember this book?
You used to talk about
it all the time!"

"Look, your words
are right inside.
See?"

Well, maybe that wasn't the right spot after all.

"Oh, hi Enzo.
What do you have here?
Your favorite alphabet toy?
What a clever idea,
but I don't think we'll
find the runaway
words here either."

Sweet little guy. . .
he's just not as
good at finding
words as I am.

Oh! I know, I know!!! The radio! Yes. . Charlie loves
music. His words are there, I just know it!

"Charlie - it's your favorite song!!!
Let's sing and dance! Sing with me!
Come on!"

Well now I'm a little stumped.
I need to think . . . .

"Oh hi, Sam."

"Hi Addi.
What are
you doing?"

"I'm looking for Charlie's words. He lost them.
I have to help him find them."

"Ohhhh. . . Hmm. . . well my mom says coffee helps her talk in the mornings. Personally, I like lemonade. You should try giving him some lemonade. And a cookie. Then maybe he can find his words. Works for me every time."

"Oh wow. I hadn't thought of that. Charlie loves cookies and lemonade! Maybe it will work!"

"Isn't it good Charlie??
Don't you want to TELL me how good it is??"

"What's that Enzo? You're a witch and you're going to cast a spell to bring his words back?? Ok. . . sure, I guess it's worth a try."

"Don't worry. Maybe it just wasn't the right spell. You can keep working on it and we'll try again."

You know, I better check at school! Maybe Charlie left his words in his desk or his backpack.

Well, there's a LOT of stuff in here, but I don't see his words.

Wow. Finding words is hard.

EUREKA! I know just what to do! Why didn't I think of this before??

I will write Santa Claus and ask him to bring Charlie his words for Christmas.

Santa can do anything!

Oh no. . . Even Santa said he doesn't have Charlie's words. I don't know where else to look. I just want my brother to be able to talk to me, to our family, to everyone.

How do I
tell Charlie I
couldn't find
his words?

"Oh, hi Charlie."

"I love you, too Charlie."

"Well, look at that. I guess we found your words after all."